Dealing with Feeling...
Angry

Isabel Thomas

Illustrated by Clare Elsom

Heinemann
LIBRARY

Chicago, Illinois

© 2013 Heinemann Library
an imprint of Capstone Global Library, LLC
Chicago, Illinois

To contact Capstone Global Library please
phone 800-747-4992, or visit our website
www.capstonepub.com

Edited by Dan Nunn, Rebecca Rissman, and
  Catherine Veitch
Designed by Philippa Jenkins
Original illustrations © Clare Elsom
Illustrated by Clare Elsom
Production by Victoria Fitzgerald
Originated by Capstone Global Library, Ltd.
Printed in China

16 15 14 13 12
10 9 8 7 6 5 4 3 2 1

**Library of Congress Cataloging-in-Publication
Data**
Thomas, Isabel, 1980-
  Angry / Isabel Thomas.
    p. cm.—(Dealing with feeling)
  Includes bibliographical references and index.
  ISBN 978-1-4329-7103-8 (hb)—ISBN 978-1-4329-
7112-0 (pb) 1. Anger in children—Juvenile literature.
2. Anger—Juvenile literature. I. Title.
  BF723.A4T56 2013
  152.4'7—dc23   2012008275

Contents

Some words are shown in bold, **like this.** Find out what they mean in the glossary on page 23.

What Is Anger?

Anger is a **feeling**. It is normal to have many kinds of feelings every day.

Everyone feels angry sometimes. We might feel angry when something hurts us, annoys us, or seems unfair.

How Do We Know When Someone Is Angry?

Our faces and bodies can show other people how we feel inside. **Feelings** can change the way that people behave, too.

Some people get quiet or cry when they are angry. Other people may shout, or try to hurt people or break things.

What Does Anger Feel Like?

Anger can make you feel hot and shaky inside. You might feel as if the anger is trapped inside your body, waiting to burst out.

It can be easy to get angry. It can be harder to stop being angry. Trying to hide angry **feelings** can make you feel worse.

Is It Okay to Feel Angry?

Two children
at a time

When somebody else breaks the rules,
it can make you lose your temper.
Many people feel angry when
something is unfair.

It is okay to feel angry, but it is not okay to hurt people. You need to find a safe way to let anger out.

Two children at a time

How Can I Deal with Anger?

Getting in trouble for something that you did not do can make you feel angry. It is okay to feel angry, but it is not okay to shout at people.

The best way to deal with **feelings** is to talk about them. You could tell the person who made you angry how you feel.

What If I Am Too Angry to Talk?

When someone makes fun of you, it can make you feel upset. It is okay to feel angry, but it is not okay to **damage** other people's things.

Find a safe way to let your anger out. You could scribble on scrap paper or tear up old newspaper.

What Are Safe Ways to Let Anger Out?

It can be **frustrating** to not be the winner. It is okay to feel bad, but it is not okay to punch, kick, or throw things.

Exercise is a safe way to let anger out. You could go for a run or a walk, or jump up and down.

How Can I Help Myself Calm Down?

When something you have made gets broken, you might feel angry. It is okay to feel grumpy, but it is not okay to fight.

Calm down by walking away. Try taking ten deep breaths. You could drink a glass of water to cool yourself down.

How Can I Help Someone Else Who Is Angry?

Everyone feels angry sometimes, even grown-ups. Sometimes angry people are not nice to other people, because they are feeling bad inside.

When they calm down, they might want to talk about how they feel. You can help by listening.

Make an Anger Toolbox

Write down some tips to help you deal with angry **feelings.**

Scribble on some paper, and then tear it up into tiny pieces.

Have a cool drink.

Take ten deep breaths.

Look at nice pictures or listen to music.

Take time out.

Talk to somebody you trust about how you feel.

Draw a picture to show what made you angry.

Stamp your feet or run outside.

Don't be afraid to ask for help. Everyone needs help sometimes.

Glossary

damage do harm to something

feeling something that happens inside our minds. It can affect our bodies and the way we behave.

frustrating something that makes us feel upset or annoyed because we cannot change it

Find Out More

Books

Bang, Molly. *When Sophie Gets Angry—Really, Really Angry.* New York: Scholastic, 2007.

Bingham, Jane. *Angry (Everybody Feels).* New York: Crabtree, 2008.

Internet sites

Facthound offers a safe, fun way to find Internet sites related to this book. All of the sites on Facthound have been researched by our staff.

Here's all you do:
Visit www.facthound.com
Type in this code: 9781432971038

Index